AR 5•7   970L

ISLE ROYALE NATIONAL PARK

A TRUE BOOK

by

Joan Kalbacken

Children's Press®
A Division of Grolier Publishing
New York London Hong Kong Sydney
Danbury, Connecticut

To Norm for his patience, love and thoughtful critiques.

Reading Consultant
Linda Cornwell
Learning Resource Consultant
Indiana Department of
Education

Isle Royale National Park includes the large island, Isle Royale, plus 200 smaller islands.

Library of Congress Cataloging-in-Publication Data

Kalbacken, Joan.
    Isle Royale National Park / by Joan Kalbacken.
        p.   cm.   —   (A true book)
    Includes index.
    Summary: Describes the history, landscape, and wildlife of the oldest, largest, and only island national park in the United States.
    ISBN 0-516-20131-X (lib. bdg.)   ISBN 0-516-26101-0 (pbk.)
    1. Isle Royale National Park (Mich.) — Juvenile literature.   2. Natural history—Michigan—Isle Royale National Park—Juvenile literature.
    [1. Isle Royale National Park (Mich.) 2. National parks and reserves.]
    I. Title. II. Series.
    F572.I8K35   1996
    917.74 '9970443—dc20   96-5294
                                                                            CIP
                                                                            AC

Contents

Isle Royale National Park

 The only island national park in the United States covers 842 square miles (1,355 square kilometers) of unspoiled wilderness with forests, harbors, lakes, and ponds. It is called Isle Royale. The French name means,

"King's Island." And Isle Royale lives up to its name.

The park lies in the northern part of Lake Superior, which is one of the Great Lakes. Isle Royale is closer to Canada than to the United States. Although it is part of the state of Michigan, it is 45 miles (72 km) from Michigan's Keweenaw Peninsula, but it is only 15 miles (24 km) from Canada.

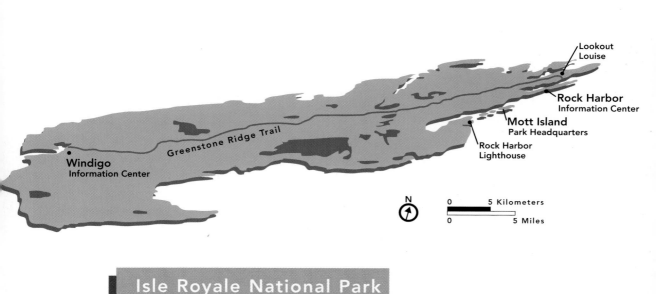

Lookout
Louise

Rock Harbor
Information Center

Mott Island
Park Headquarters

Rock Harbor
Lighthouse

Greenstone Ridge Trail

Windigo
Information Center

N

0   5 Kilometers

0   5 Miles

Isle Royale National Park

   Isle Royale National Park is an archipelago of more than 200 islands. The big island— Isle Royale—is about 45 miles (72 km) long and 9 miles (14 km) wide. Five chains of islands and several peninsulas form deep harbors.

7

Where is Isle Royale?

Isle Royale National Park is part of the state of Michigan. The park itself is located on the large island called Isle Royale. There are about two hundred tiny islands that surround it. The island was claimed by French explorers, who named it in honor of their king, Louis XIV. Visitors to the park can hike to an ancient copper mining pit or canoe through the streams and coves.

ISLE ROYAL NATIONAL PARK

CANADA
U.S.

Ontario

Lake Superior

Keweenaw Peninsula

Minnesota

Wisconsin

Lake Huron

Iowa

Lake Michigan

MICHIGAN

Ontario

Illinois

Indiana

Lake Erie

Ohio

How Was Isle Royale Formed?

Thousands of years ago, a volcano erupted in what is now the Lake Superior region. The flow of lava hardened and formed the first rocks of Isle Royale. Later, a glacier buried the island under a huge ice sheet. When the ice melted,

9

Huge glaciers carved the islands of Isle Royale.

Lake Superior kept the islands hidden beneath its waters. Gradually, the water level of the lake lowered and the island's rocky ridges appeared above the icy waters. Over a long period of time, small particles of soil settled on the rocks, and trees and flowers started to grow. In many places, the soil on Isle Royale still measures only a few inches deep.

Early Visitors

No one knows who first lived on Isle Royale, but American Indians mined copper there about 4,000 years ago.

The area was called the United States Chippewa Territory until the middle of the 1600s because the Chippewa, or Ojibwa, indians

The Chippewa had settled on Isle Royale long before French explorers arrived.

lived there. Then, in 1669, the islands of Isle Royale were claimed by French explorers. Hunters later arrived looking for fur-bearing animals. In the 1700s, the Hudson's Bay Company and the American Fur Company came to the

Hunters set traps on Isle Royale to catch fur-bearing animals.

island to set traps for beaver. The islands became part of the United States in 1783.

By the early 1900s, a few families had settled on Isle Royale; but Albert Stoll, a Detroit journalist, thought the wilderness should remain unspoiled. He led an effort to make the area a national park and in 1931, the United States government established the islands as a national park.

People come to Isle Royale to study its natural setting and its wildlife.

Many quiet, peaceful trails guide visitors through the park.

A national park gives protection and shelter to wildlife. On Isle Royale, there are no roads, so there is no traffic. Visitors follow peaceful trails and enjoy the natural beauty of the wilderness.

Getting There

You can get to Isle Royale National Park only by boat or seaplane. Perhaps this is why Isle Royale has fewer visitors than any other national park in the United States. The National Park Service runs a ship called the *Ranger III* from Michigan's Upper Peninsula.

Visitors prepare to board *Ranger III* for their trip to the park (above). The *Sky Ranger* (inset) flies to Isle Royale from Houghton, Michigan.

Ranger III makes the round trip twice a week during the summer. Privately owned ships also carry passengers to the park from June until September. In good summer weather, float-planes fly to Isle Royale daily. The seaplane, *Sky Ranger*, also makes frequent flights from Houghton, Michigan.

Isle Royale has no telephone service. In an emergency, the park's radio system is the only way to contact the mainland. The only available two-way radios are on Mott Island and at Windigo Ranger Station.

Hudson's Bay Company

The Hudson's Bay Company was formed in 1670. Its purpose was to get furs from North America and sell them in Europe. American Indian hunters and trappers brought beaver pelts and

other animal furs to the company's trading posts, one of which was on Isle Royale. In exchange, the Indians were given guns, beads, cloth, blankets, and utensils. Originally, the company operated around Hudson Bay and spread westward to the Pacific Ocean. Today, more than three hundred years later, the Hudson's Bay Company is still in business.

The Trails

More than 170 miles (274 km) of foot trails wind through Isle Royale. The main trail, called Greenstone Ridge, follows the length of the main island, running 40 miles (64 km) from the lodge at Rock Harbor to Washington Harbor. The trail bends and twists through

A flowering meadow along Greenstone Ridge trail (above), Rocky inlets along the shores of the main island (right)

forests, flowered meadows, wet swamps, and rocky cliffs. Rocky inlets line the shore. Farther inland, twisting streams lead to peaceful lakes.

Among the park's most unique sights is Monument Rock. This huge rock—carved by waves, rain, and ice—towers about 70 feet (21 meters) high.

American Indians used Lookout Louise to see for miles offshore. Visitors can see the same beautiful view today.

Monument Rock (right); the view of Canada from Lookout Louise (below)

The Ojibway Lookout tower also offers a spectacular view of Canada.

From the Ojibway Lookout, you can see all the way to Canada—15 miles (24 km). And from Washington Creek

Trail, hikers can explore the remains of an old copper mining pit at Windigo.

Another trail leads to old Rock Harbor Lighthouse, built in 1885. Its light guided miners, trappers, and traders to the shores of Rock Harbor. Not far from the old lighthouse, the Rock Harbor Lodge has rooms and cabins for visitors who come to hike, fish, study the environment, or just enjoy the wilderness.

Rock Harbor Lighthouse was built in 1885.

The Weather

The weather at Isle Royale is usually quite cool. In summer, the temperature seldom reaches 80 degrees Fahrenheit (27 degrees Celsius). The evenings are cool. Mornings are sometimes foggy, and strong winds blow from Lake Superior over the islands. The water is often too rough for

The water around Isle Royale is often too rough for boats or seaplanes to land (left). Thick fog sometimes forms over Isle Royale on cool mornings (right).

boats or seaplanes to carry people to the park. Winters are so cold that visitors are not permitted.

Plants and Animals

The park's isolation from the mainland means that the air and water are very clean because there is no pollution. That makes it an ideal habitat for wildflowers. Due to the cold temperatures, plants grow slowly; but many kinds of flowers grow on the islands. In summer, yellow

Yellow lady's-slippers (above) and calypso orchids (left) bloom during the summer.

lady's-slippers bloom along-side the swamp candle and purple loosestrife. Purple-fringed orchids grow along the trails. Across the isle, hardy cedar and tamarack trees grow in the swamps and bogs. Birch, balsam, maple, poplar, and many types of evergreen trees flourish along the drier trails.

The isle's wildlife includes squirrels, red foxes, beavers, muskrat, mink, weasels, snowshoe hare, and moose. But how did these animals get to islands that were covered first, by a huge glacier and, later, surrounded by water?

Scientists are still unsure about how all of the isle's

Isle Royale is home to (clockwise from left) moose, hare, beavers, mink, and foxes.

mammals arrived at the park. But they are sure that there were no moose on the main island before 1900. Then, during the bitterly cold winter of 1912, Lake Superior froze. The moose probably walked 15 miles (24 km) across the thick ice from Canada. On Isle Royale, the moose found tender brush and tasty plants and thrived in the new land. Eventually, moose herds increased to the point where there was not enough food for all of them. Scientists estimate that at least three thousand moose lived on the main island in 1930, but most of them starved to death within a few years.

Lake Superior froze again in the winter of 1948. This time, timber wolves found their way across the ice from Canada. These natural predators of the moose arrived just in time to save the remaining moose from starving due to overpopulation. Now, neither the moose herds nor the wolf

packs are too large. Bear, deer, skunks, or porcupine have never been seen on these islands.

Many beautiful birds have also found their way to this wildlife sanctuary. Herring gulls, with gray-and-white feathers and black-tipped wings, are seen along the shores. More than 50 kinds of fish live in the lakes and inland streams. Bald eagles nest along the rocky cliffs. Osprey, ravens, woodpeckers, and many kinds of warblers also make Isle Royale their home.

Herring gulls (below left) are abundant on Isle Royale. Bald eagles (right) and woodpeckers (below right) live in the vast forests of the park.

Park Restrictions

Keeping Isle Royale clean and unspoiled requires visitors to follow a few rules. There are no trash cans in the wilderness, and hikers on the trails are not allowed to bury, burn, or scatter trash. They must carry their own trash out of the park. To prevent the

Hikers enjoy a rest along one of the park's trails.

wildlife from becoming dependent upon people, visitors are not permitted to feed the animals. You cannot bring a pet to Isle Royale. Pets might carry diseases and infect or scare the wildlife. Visitors must be very quiet. Hikers may sleep overnight in the screened, three-sided shelters along the trails, but they must be absolutely quiet from ten o'clock at night until six o'clock in the morning. Visitors may not bring guns, fireworks, or portable stereos to Isle Royale.

Visitors to the island often stay overnight in these shelters.

Nature's Laboratory

Isle Royale National Park has been the setting for many valuable research projects. Biologists and other scientists have studied the park's plant and animal life through ground and aerial surveys. The natural sciences help us understand how things work

Scientists conduct many studies at Isle Royale (top). The sun rises over Isle Royale National Park (right).

in our environment. Isle Royale National Park, an island wilderness, is also a national treasure.

To Find Out More

Here are some additional resources to help you learn more about Isle Royale National Park:

 **Books**

 **Organizations**

Crump, Donald J., ed. **Adventures in Your National Parks**. National Geographic, 1989.

Fradin, Dennis. **Michigan.** Children's Press, 1994.

Mead, Robin. **Our National Parks.** Smithmark, 1993.

Weber, Michael. **Our National Parks.** Millbrook, 1994.

Isle Royale National Park
800 East Lake Shore Drive
Houghton, MI 49931
906-482-0984

National Park Service
Office of Public Inquiries
P.O. Box 37127
Washington, DC 20013
202-208-4747

National Parks and Conservation Association
1776 Massachusetts
  Avenue, NW
Washington, DC 20036
1-800-NAT-PARK
natparks@aol.com
npca@npca.org

Online Sites

Great Outdoor Recreation Pages (GORP)

http://www.gorp.com/gorp/resource/US_National_Park/main.htm

Information on hiking, fishing, boating, climate, places to stay, plant life, wildlife, and more.

National Park Foundation

CompuServe offers online maps, park products, special programs, a question-and-answer series, and in-depth information available by park name, state, region, or interest. From the main menu, select *Travel*, then *Where To Go*, then *Complete Guide to America's National Parks.*

National Park Service World Wide Web Server

http://www.nps.gov

Includes virtual tours, maps, essays.

National Parks Magazine

editorial@npca.org

Focuses on the park system in general, as well as on individual sites.

Note: Many of the national parks have their own home pages on the World Wide Web. Do some exploring!

Important Words

archipelago group of islands

floatplane airplane that can float on water

glacier mass of ice found in very cold water

inlet rocky creeks along the shore of an island

isolation separate; alone

overpopulation too crowded

peninsula land that is almost completely surrounded by water

predator animal that hunts and kills other animals

sanctuary refuge; safe place

seaplane airplane that can take off and land on water

unspoiled unharmed, not damaged

Index

(**Boldface** page numbers
indicate illustrations.)

Meet the Author

Joan Kalbacken was raised on a farm in northwest Wisconsin. She graduated from the University of Wisconsin, Madison, and completed graduate work at Coe College, Iowa; the University of Toulouse, France; and Illinois State University, Normal. She taught Mathematics and French in Illinois for twenty-nine years and is the author of several books for Children's Press. Ms. Kalbacken is also the recipient of a Distinguished Illinois Author Award from the Illinois Reading Council.